Beginner's (
Stock Market |

Secrets of Stock Trading Revealed – Comprehensive Guides to Stock Market Investing and Bulletproof Strategies To Maximize Profit While Minimizing the Risk

---

Marcus De LaRoy

Disclaimer

This is for entertainment and educational purposes only, not actual stock advice, for legal purposes. Please note that for advice specific to each individual's financial situation, they should seek out a professional investment advisor.

Table of Contents

Introduction..1

Chapter One : Understanding Stocks...................................3

Chapter Two : How To Get Started With Stocks 23

Chapter Three : Passive investment through ETFs..........................39

Chapter Four : How To Create Passive Income Through Dividend Investing..54

Chapter Five : Warren Buffett, Value Investing, & P/E Ratios........64

Chapter Six : Growth Investing Strategy.........................72

Chapter Seven : Building Your Portfolio 81

Chapter Eight : Common Mistakes Young Investors Make............95

Final Words...101

Introduction

Coming up with a way to generate more money is the goal for almost everyone. Investing is one of the greatest means of getting your money to work for you to create a clear path towards achieving financial independence.

The stock market is one of the best options you can use to invest your money. Are you ready to learn the tips and tricks of how to invest your money in the stock market? You can utilize the different stock investment strategies to grow your money. Even with minimal risks, you can still make profits.

In this book, you will learn everything you need to know in order to start making money by buying and selling stocks today. These steps help you avoid gambling with your hard-earned money. We will look at the fundamentals of stock market investing and the long-term strategies you can follow as a beginner investor to grow your money.

You will also be able to avoid some of the pitfalls and costly mistakes other beginner investors make. The book provides you with a simple road map on how to invest in stocks.

Some of the topics you will learn in this book include;

What the stock market is, how it works, and how you should invest in it.

Why it is important to have a broker or financial advisor to help you make smart decisions on the stock market.

How to select the best investment account.

How to buy stocks and how to pick the best stocks like Warren Buffet.

How to diversify your investment portfolio and earn long-term investment returns via exchange-traded funds (ETFs).

The best trading strategies to build the right stock market portfolio that help you meet your investment goals.

How to generate passive income through value investing and growth investing strategies.

How to reassess and rebalance your investment portfolio with the right asset classes.

·Some of the tips and tricks beginners can follow to start making money

Even without any knowledge about the stock market, this guide will help you get started in investing and trading appropriately. Join other investors and learn how to control investment risks and available options you can utilize to grow your wealth! This book will help you start trading in the stock market in no time.

Chapter One

Understanding Stocks

Investing in stocks is one of the greatest ways to gaining financial independence. Investing in stocks helps you put some money aside and let it work for you so that you can reap the benefits in the future. Your goal for investing in the stock market is the potential for high returns.

Just like other types of investments, price fluctuations of stocks over time and other external factors you have no control over can affect your earnings. One needs to take advantage of the stock increases to diversify your investments.

There are a lot of horror stories about investors losing about 50% of their investment portfolio. This makes some investors approach the stock market with fear, especially those with limited experience.

It is important to know that the stock market carries a lot of risks. That is why you have to approach the stock market with a lot of discipline. When approached in a professional manner, the stock market is the most efficient means of building your net worth.

Experienced investors rely on a variety of strategies to build their wealth from the stock market. Some may look for long-term trading options, while others are actively involved and trade more frequently.

In order to understand how the stock market works, let's begin by defining what a stock is and the different types of stocks you can invest in.

What are stocks?

Stocks act as a financial instrument that represents your ownership of shares in a company. By becoming a shareholder in the company, you have the right to receive part of the company's earnings. This is a great way for beginner investors to build wealth.

When you buy stocks of a company, you have the right to residual claims on the capital gains and losses of that company. This is because you own a fraction of the company's total assets. Companies that are consistently able to beat expected earnings per share during quarterly reports are those whose stock prices rise and provide shareholders with long-term profits.

You will also have the right to receive dividends from the company's revenue. A lot of the companies pay dividends on a quarterly basis.

Alternatively, you can earn your return on investment by selling the stocks for a profit. Stock prices appreciate over time, so you can hold your shares and sell them when the prices go up.

re are two types of stocks;

·Common shareholder

·Preferred shareholder

If you're a common shareholder, you have voting rights to participate in the annual general meetings of that company and receive dividends.

While preferred shareholders have limited rights to vote in the shareholder meetings, they do receive dividends payouts and in an event of liquidation. They have the right to receive a claim on the assets of the company.

How to buy stocks

Companies can raise money through the sale of company shares. The company uses the money to expand its business operation, pay off debts, invest in a new product line, or fund various operations of the business.

When a private limited company wants to access a large amount of capital, it can do so by going public through the initial public offering (IPO) process. The company hires an investment bank that uses valuation techniques to determine the market value of the company, the number of shares to be offered to the public, and at what price.

The stocks of the company become available to the public, and investors can buy or sell them on the stock exchange. This converts a privately traded firm with few shareholders to a publicly traded firm held by several members of the general public.

The investors of the publicly traded firm get an opportunity to gain from the earnings of the company.

Once the company's stocks are on the market, investors can easily buy them. If you want to buy the stocks, you can buy them directly from the company or through a stock exchange.

Investors who sell their stocks do so through a Stock Exchange (SE) Company like the New York Stock Exchange (NYSE). A SE acts as a secondary market that allows existing shareholders to sell their shares to potential buyers.

After the price of shares listed in the SE is set, the trading can start. The prices of the shares keep on fluctuating depending on a number of factors such as demand, supply, and other variables that affect the prices of the stocks.

Typically, most investors use a brokerage account to buy and sell their stocks. When trading through the broker's online trading platform, the brokers determine the buying price (the bid) and selling price (offer or ask) of the stocks.

How the prices of shares are set

The stock price is the current market price at which a share of stock is trading. When the shares of a publicly traded firm are issued to the public, a price per share reflects the value of the firm.

A company determines the amount of money they want to raise during the initial public offering, that combined with the total number of shares they are offering to the public and the value of the company, determines the initial stock price offer. The set price can rise or fall depending on a number of internal and external factors, which are discussed below.

In addition, trader sentiment can also influence the share price of the stocks. They rely on the financial metric to determine the firm's value, market changes, historical earnings of the firm, and the expected profit of the firm. This information helps traders to bid on the shares either up or down.

The aim of the traders is to make a return on their investment through;

Receiving dividends. When the firm makes profits, they pay the shareholders dividends equivalent to every share held.

Selling shares at a profit. They buy the shares when the prices are low and sell them when the prices go up.

Therefore, the stock prices depend on the *bid* to buy shares at a particular price or an *offer* (ask) to sell shares of the company at a particular price. There are different investors and traders in the market knowledgeable on the value of a specific stock, and they have a specific price they're willing to buy and sell the stocks. All these transactions are conducted through a stock exchange platform that matches the buyers with the sellers.

A stock exchange company calculates the price of shares by determining the current transaction price for the maximum number of shares. The prices change based on the buy and sell offers of the stock.

How to calculate the market price of shares

A number of factors drive the prices of stock in the marketplace. At any given moment, the stock prices are due to the demand and supply of stocks in the market. The fundamental factors drive the prices of stocks based on them;

Company's earnings such as earnings per share (EPS)

Price to earnings (P/E) ratio

Price to earnings ratio is one of the popular methods that determine the intrinsic value of the stock prices. The valuation multiple helps you determine the price you're willing to pay for the stocks that contribute to your future earnings.

A common stock owner has the right to claim on the earnings of the firm, and EPS (earning per share) will be his return on investment.

Traders rely on the last updated value of the company's shares and multiply this figure with the outstanding shares to determine how valuable the company is.

You can also calculate the price of shares using the price-to-earnings ratio (P/E ratio) method.

Intrinsic stock value=P/E ratio * Earning per share.

The stock price not only reflects the current value of the company but also reflects the company's prospects and the expected growth of the company in the future.

Quantitative techniques like **dividend discount models** (DDMs) can predict the company's share price trajectory. This technique operates on the concept that the current stock price is equal to the total sum of future dividend payments when it is discounted back to the present value.

The dividend discount model relies on the time value of money (TVM) theory to determine the company shares using the total sum of the expected future dividends.

The Gordon growth model

One of the most commonly used dividend discount models is the *Gordon growth model* developed by Myron Gordon, which states that:

Present value of stock= (dividend per share) / (discount rate-growth rate)

$P=D1/r\text{-}g$

Where,

P= Current stock price

g= Growth rate expected for the dividends

r= rate of return

D_1= Dividend Value for the next financial year

Example: Goshen Inc. stocks are trading at $100 per share. The company requires a minimum rate of return of 5% and currently pays a $2 dividend per share to the shareholders, and this is expected to increase by 3% each year.

Intrinsic stock value: $2/ (0.05-0.03) =$100

Using the Gordon growth model, the present stock is valued at its intrinsic level. If the shares are traded at $80, they will be undervalued by $20, which is a great opportunity for investors who want to buy more stocks. But if the stocks were traded at $120 per share, they would have overvalued by $20.

Factors affecting price fluctuations of stocks

There are both internal and external factors that influence the rise and fall of stock prices in the market.

Internal factors

Some issues within the firm can result in changes in the stock prices. Some of these factors include;

1. Supply and demand of stocks

The demand and supply of stocks determine the share price. If there is high demand for certain products in the market and less supply, the prices will increase. For example, if a company issues new shares in the market, the number of shares is limited, and as more investors try to buy the limited stock of shares, it will result in low supply. In return, the price of shares increases.

If the supply of the product balances out with the product's demand, the prices may remain constant, but if the supply is greater than the demand, the prices of shares are likely to drop.

Therefore, the prices of shares depend on how unique and effective the products of the firm are. If the produced goods are of the same standards, the prices are likely to remain the same or slightly higher even when the supply is very high.

2. Changes in management and production

If there are changes in the management of the firm or production department, it can cause changes in the prices of shares. Changes in the production process, the management team, and management style can increase the effectiveness and efficiency of the firm leading to increased profits that in return increases the prices of shares.

Poor management and poor quality products can result in a decrease in share prices. The firm's profitability and its earnings affect the prices of shares.

3. Financial performance

Just like supply and demand that causes the prices to move up and down. The financial performance of the firm is an important factor that contributes to the increased demand for shares.

This is because stocks that earn more money are more valuable to investors. If the company earns more money than what the investors expected, it will be in high demand.

A company with good earnings both during good and bad economic conditions will result in high demand for the stock. The consistency and stability of the company will encourage a stream of buyers to the company's stocks, and this keeps the price of stocks very high.

4. Industry performance

Often, stock prices in industry-related companies tend to move in tandem with each other. This is because the companies experience the same market conditions and changes. However, a single piece of bad news can affect the stock prices of the company, and the other competing companies in the same market can take advantage of that.

5. Investors opinions

Investor's opinions and sentiments concerning the company can affect the stock market, and this causes the stock prices to go up and down. The market can affect the value of stocks in two ways;

Bull market: In this form of market, investors have confidence over the stock market, leading to increased prices of stocks. This usually occurs during the economic recovery stage or the boom stage.

Bear market: This is usually associated with a weak market where investors have little confidence in the market. This lowers the stock prices, and it mostly happens during the recession period. The market is characterized by a high unemployment period and increased prices of commodities.

External factors

6. Economic trends

The performance of the general economy is one of the macroeconomic factors that affect the price of shares. If the economy is going through a period of recession, some companies, no matter how great they are, may find it difficult to make money.

During this period, more companies record a reduced growth rate, and some end up making losses. In this phase of the economy, the demand for stocks is very low. And since the supply of stocks exceeds the demand, the prices go down. Any increase in the demand for stocks will drive the prices up.

7. Interest rates

World Banks operate on monetary policy where it raises or lowers the interest rates in order to stabilize the economy. For example, if a firm borrows money at a high-interest rate to fund its business operations or for expansion, it will affect the cost of its debts. This reduces the firm's profits and lowers dividends paid to the shareholders. As a result, the price of stocks drops.

8. Inflation

Inflation is a huge driver that affects the valuation of stocks. The rate of inflation determines the profitability of the firm; a higher inflation slows sales and reduces firm profitability. While a low inflation rate will result in increased profitability of the firm.

When banks raise interest rates to lower inflation, it increases consumer prices. These changes reduce the price of stocks in the market.

9. Deflation

This is another factor that reduces the pricing power for companies. When the prices fall, it reduces the firm's profits and economic activity. As a result, investors start selling their stocks and use the proceeds from sales to invest in fixed-income investments such as bonds.

Banks may reduce the interest rates to encourage people to borrow more money and spend more. The goal of deflation is to increase economic activity through more spending.

Market capitalization

Market capitalization (market cap) represents the current market value of the company. Investors can easily determine the company's worth by taking the company's stock prices multiplied by the number of outstanding shares.

Market capitalization = current share price*total outstanding shares

Any change in the stock prices will result in changes to the company's market cap. Investors often use the market cap to rank the company and compare its performance with that of other industry peers. This is the reason why investors are so keen on the stock prices because any drop of stock price by $0.1 will result in a loss of $100,000 if the shareholder has 1 million shares.

Stocks are often based on the respective market value. For example;

Large-cap: Companies classify a large market value of above $10 billion as a large-cap stock.

Mid-cap: This represents companies with a market value of less than $10 billion. This market cap is more volatile and is associated with growth-oriented stocks.

Small cap: This represents companies in the growth stage and has a stock value of less than $1 billion. Companies in this class experience high risks and high returns on stocks. Most companies belong to this category of market cap and have greater growth opportunities than large-cap companies.

The market capitalization and company classification provide investors with a metric to determine which stocks to buy, how to diversify their portfolio, and how to make smart investment decisions. Companies with large market cap have more assets and offer a consistent increase in dividends payments and share value than those with small-cap. However, large-cap companies provide a huge return on investment over the long run.

Stock market returns

Long-term investment in stocks is the key to making more money from your investment. The main goal is to save money you don't need for at least five years. If you're looking for short-term strategies, you should look for lower-risk strategies but expect to earn lower returns from them.

How long you hold your stocks before selling them determines your stock performance. Thus, if you move in and out of the stock market more often, then you will not be able to realize all of your potential annual returns. So to make more money in stocks, you have to stay invested.

Generally, the historical stock market return is usually10% per annum. The volatility of the stock market makes returns vary from one year to the next. It is not easy to predict which year the stock returns will be above average or below average.

S&P 500

Typically, when analysts talk about the "average stock market return," they are referring to the annual return of the S&P 500 index. The S&P 500 index is a benchmark for measuring stock market performance. It is a market-weighted index that consists of about 500 publicly traded companies in America. For nearly a century, the annual average stock return after the adoption of the S&P 500 is approximately 10%.

Though 10% is the historical average annual return, actual annual returns can vary widely based on market conditions. One contributing factor to this variability is the inflation rate. Each year, investors should expect a loss of about 2% to 3% after the adjustment for inflation. However, inflation itself can also be variable.

Another problem that affects retail investor returns is the time at which you decide to enter the market. For example, investors who buy stocks when the prices are at the lows of a bear market and sell when the market prices are high during bull markets will have higher returns than investors who don't take advantage of the significant discounts they can purchase stocks at during bear markets or moments of market weakness. Therefore, the timing for your next stock purchase plays a big role in determining your returns.

Dow Jones Industrial Average

Dow Jones Industrial Average (DJIA) is a stock market index that tracks the performance of 30 major companies listed in the US stock exchange. It is one of the commonly used market indexes for blue-chip companies with stable returns.

The performance of the companies listed in the DJIA is based on the overall growth rate in the economy. For example, Microsoft Corporation and Walt Disney have a strong economic impact compared to other weakly performing companies.

As the economy keeps on changing, so does the Dow index composition. The Dow component is affected when a company becomes less relevant in the economy, and it can be replaced with a new company to reflect the shift.

Stocks that have higher prices are given a higher weight in the Dow index. Thus, a high percentage of market capitalization will result in a move to a high-priced component that influences the final calculated value.

Buy and hold investing strategy

The buy and hold is a long-term investment strategy where investors buy high-quality stocks and hold them for long periods of time regardless of price fluctuations in the market. This strategy is ideal for investors interested in healthy long-term stock returns and not bothered by the short-term price movement.

Investors using the buy hold strategy believe that the long-term returns will be able to withstand the market volatility associated with short-term returns. Thus, your "time in the market" is more important than "timing for the perfect market".

When an investor buys and holds stocks with the expectation that they will rise in value is said to have *long positions* because he owns the shares bought. Whereas an investor with *short positions* doesn't actually own the shares yet.

Buying long

Buying long is a long positioning investment strategy where investors buy stocks and hold them. It is an investment practice in the capital market where investors are not planning to sell the stocks in the near future.

If you're expecting to benefit from upward price movement, then you should go for long positioning. The stock value appreciates with time. Therefore, the investors don't have to keep watching the market. Though there are situations that make the shares drop, like the current world Covid-19 pandemic that has led to the global fall of equity markets.

In addition, a prolonged bear market can also affect your long positioning investment strategy.

Short selling

Short selling or short positioning is a classic strategy that focuses on the perfect timing of the stock market as the market transitions from high prices to lower prices. The strategy can be profitable if proper risk management strategies are followed during the uptrends and downtrends.

A short-selling strategy requires a simple laid down plan for entry to the market, perfect timing, and coming up with a defensive trade management strategy. Traders should be very careful when using this approach.

Short selling requires traders to employ a short positioning strategy where they sell their shares first and repurchase them back when the prices reduce. If investors believe that the price of shares is likely to fall in the future, they short sell their shares.

When a short position is in place, investors often borrow shares from an investment bank or a financial institution of their choice. However, they have to pay the borrowing fee in order to short sell.

With a short positioning strategy, you have a high potential to earn more profits or end up making uncapped losses. Some investors jump into the stock market to buy stock and sell them when there is greed in the stock market. Be careful when using this trading technique.

Always take advantage of the bull and bear market to maximize your profits.

How to take advantage of bull and bear markets

The terms 'bull' and 'bear' describe the market conditions. That is, whether the stock market is appreciating in value or depreciating. The performance of the stock market is very important in determining your stock investment portfolio.

Therefore, you should evaluate how each of the two market conditions influences your investment decisions. Investor's attitudes and how they feel about the current economic trends influence the financial market.

The bull market

A bull market is characterized by an aggressive rise in stock prices over a period of time. When the stock prices start to rise, there is a lot of greed for the stocks and more people are willing to invest in stocks.

More investors are willing to buy stocks and benefit from the upward trend, but there is less supply of stocks. As a result, the investors will compete for the available stocks leading to increased prices.

Investors have faith that the economy will continue on an uptrend path over a long time. High employment levels and performance of the economy are the main contributors to the bull market.

The bear market

During the bear market, the stock market is declining in value and investors get more scared in investing their money because the stock prices become more volatile. In most cases, the investors may decide to withdraw their money from the bear market and wait until the downward trend reverses.

The demand for stocks is lower and more investors are looking forward to selling their shares instead of buying. And as a result, the share prices drop.

During this downward trend, there is slow economic growth and a high unemployment rate as companies start laying off workers.

Chapter Summary

Stocks are a great way for the company to raise capital. When a privately traded company wants to access a large capital base, it can do so by going public through an IPO process.

The price of every share in a publicly-traded company is a reflection of the company's value and determines the amount the members of the public are willing to pay to gain a portion of the company. The prices of the shares can rise or drop depending on various factors within and outside the firm. These factors affect the effectiveness and efficiency of the firm.

Individuals investors rely on the market value and classification to determine the best stocks to buy. Generally, the average annual stock market returns are usually 10%. But the volatility of the stock market makes it hard to determine when the returns will be above average or below average.

In the next chapter, you will learn how to get started with stocks.

Chapter Two

How To Get Started With Stocks

Stock investment is one of the greatest means of growing your money over the long term. However, as a beginner investor, you may find the stock market intimidating because the prices of stocks keep on rising and falling often. Thus, without sufficient knowledge of stocks, you may end up losing a lot of your hard-earned money.

Educating yourself on how the stock market works will help you make the right investment choices. A stock market allows potential investors to buy and sell securities, individual company stakes, and exchange-traded funds (ETFs).

The stock exchange market is subject to government rules and regulations. It also has its own rules that govern its operations. Although there are different stock exchange systems where stocks are traded, the New York Stock Exchange (NYSE) and Nasdaq are the best stock exchange systems in the world. Other stock exchange systems include the Tokyo Stock Exchange, Shanghai Stock Exchange, and Hong Kong Stock Exchange.

Stock analysts use indexes to determine the overall performance of the market. The indexes help measure the weighted average value from various securities. For example, the S&P 500, Dow Jones Industrial Average (DJIA), and Nasdaq are the major indexes for measuring stock performance in the market. The rise and fall of the index value indicate the change in the average value of stocks held within the index.

Therefore, learning how the stock market works and how to control your emotions when trading can help you can build long-term wealth. You will be surprised how an investment in the S&P 500 index can become worth millions over time.

You should learn the basics about investing in stocks before you commit your money to this type of investment. If you're a beginner, this guide will provide you with the knowledge you need to jumpstart your stock investment journey.

The steps to follow include;

1. Determine your investment goals

2. Start your investment journey

3. Decide how much to invest in stocks

4. Open an investment account

5. Choose stocks to buy

6. Set up your budget

7. Continue investing

8. Manage your stock portfolio

Step 1: Determine your investment goals

Before you begin your investment journey, you need to evaluate your overall financial status and whether you have enough money to accommodate a new project.

When determining your financial goals, you should evaluate yourself in terms of employment status, debts, the size of your family, and your household budget.

As you consider your goals ask yourself, why do you want to start investing?

Are you looking forward to investing for your retirement?

Are you setting aside money for short-term goals?

How much risk are you willing to take to pursue your goal?

Asking yourself these questions will help shape your investment decisions. You don't have to be a pro in stock market investing to answer these simple questions. Having knowledge about your finances helps you decide how to best invest your money.

Step 2. Start your investment journey

Come up with ways on how you're going to invest in stocks. What kind of investor are you? Some investors decide to buy shares on an individual stock, while others decide to choose a less active approach.

Which of the following statements describes you?

I'm an analytical person, and I like working with numbers and researching.

I spend several hours each week researching about the stock market

I like reading on how to invest in different stocks, but I hate math and don't want to dive into any math-related tasks.

I am busy and don't have enough time to analyze the stocks.

No matter which statement describes your personality, with basics on stock investment, you can become an excellent investor. You will only need to know "how."

Different ways you can invest in the stock market

1. Individual stocks

If you have enough time to thoroughly research and analyze stocks on a regular basis, you can invest in individual stocks. But if you don't have time to research, analyze earning reports, and do moderate calculations, then you can take a passive approach in stocks.

Taking an active approach requires you to take part in managing the growth of your money. You also have to be smart and patient in order to beat the market and grow your wealth over time.

2. Index funds

Index funds are an investment vehicle that allows investors to track the market index as well as help balance your investment portfolio.

This type of investment relies on a passive investment strategy and mimics the performance and composition of the stock market index.

Investors can also choose to engage in index funds in addition to buying individual stocks. Index funds allow you to track a stock index such as the S&P 500.

The lower costs of index funds contribute to their overall success and make them an attractive investment. Many studies have shown that a vast majority of professional money managers do not consistently beat the returns provided by a simple S&P 500 index fund over the long term.

3. Robo-advisors

Robo-advisors have been gaining popularity in recent years. They act as brokers who invest money on behalf of the investors into portfolio index funds or individual stocks. Robo advisors search for the appropriate investment portfolio based on the investor's age, risk tolerance, and goals. They not only choose the right investments for you but also optimize your tax efficiency to automatically make the changes over time.

All major brokerage firms offer low-cost investment management services to investors based on their specific goals.

4. Employer 401 (k) investment

Investing through your employer is the most common mode of investment for beginners on a tight budget. It requires investors to contribute a small percentage of their monthly salary into a retirement account. The focus is on long-term goals such as retirement.

Using work-based investment plans, the amount is deducted from your paycheck before the calculation of taxes. This makes the contribution less painful.

If you already have a 401(k) retirement account, you can start investing for your future by buying a company's stocks or investing in mutual funds.

Step 3. Decide how much to invest in stocks

Before you subject your money to risk, you should set some money aside that you can use in case of financial emergencies.

If you have money you might need in a period of less than five years, do not invest it in the stock market. Though the stock market may rise in the long run, there is too much uncertainty on stock prices within a very short period of time.

Sometimes it's normal to have a drop of about 20% of stock prices each year. Currently, as a result of the Covid-19 pandemic, the market has dropped to about 40% and expected to rise again within a few months.

Therefore, to reduce the risks associated with stock investments, you should;

Set up some emergency funds

Set money aside to fund your child's next payment for tuition

Set money aside for a down payment for your home even if you have no plans of buying a home.

Now that you have set money aside for emergencies, it is time to determine your investable money using the asset allocation concept. How much to invest depends on your age, investment goals, and risk tolerance.

As you get older, you will find that stocks are not the right investment for your money. But if you're young, you can easily dive into the ups and downs associated with the stock market. This is not the case if you're retired and depend on your investment income.

To know the percentage of your investable money to put in stocks, subtract your age from 110. This percentage includes investable money from mutual funds and stock-based ETFs. You can invest the remaining money in a fixed-income investment such as bonds and other high-yield investments. You can easily adjust this investment ratio up and down depending on your risk tolerance.

For example, if you're 40 years old, you can invest 70% of your investable money into the stock market and the remaining 30% on a fixed income. If you can take more risk and are planning to work past your retirement age, then you can increase your investment ratio in the stock market.

Step 4. Open an Investment Account

To be able to buy stocks, you must have an investment account. If you have some experience, you can go for a brokerage account, but if you need help with your investment, you can open an account with a Robo advisor.

You don't need a lot of money to open a brokerage or Robo advisors account.

Opening a brokerage account

Opening a brokerage account provides you with an easy and cost-effective means to buy stocks and other types of investments. A brokerage account provides you with a do-it-yourself (DIY) option where you research the stocks to invest in, buy and sell stocks and funds on your own.

Decide on the type of brokerage account you want to open. You can decide to open a standard brokerage account or an individual retirement account (IRA).

Your decision on what type of brokerage account to open depends on how easily you want to access your money and why you want to invest in stocks. And depending on the account you want to open, you should ask yourself the following questions:

What are the trading fees of the broker's account?

Does the brokerage provide you with banking services?

Do the brokerage offer you advisory services?

Do the broker's aims match your investment strategy?

Does the broker offer any research tools to the investor?

What can you invest with the broker, and are there any customer services provided?

For example, if you want an account that will allow you to easily access your money because you're only saving for the rainy days, then you can open a taxable standard brokerage account. The majority of investors go for a standard brokerage account and usually have an employer 401(K) account to save for their retirement.

Otherwise, if you don't have an already existing employer 401(K) retirement account, then you can go for an individual retirement account (IRA) to save up for your retirement and build up a nest egg. Though this account is tax-sheltered, you can't withdraw money from it until your retirement age. This acts as a great way to grow your money.

IRA is suitable for self-employed individuals and small business owners.

Once you have decided on what type of broker account to open, you have to choose the best online discount stock broker to work with. The brokers help you to open your online brokerage account without any initial deposit. However, once you open the account, you have to fund it in order to be able to buy investments.

Most brokerage investment firms provide a link to the banking institution to make it easy for investors to transfer money from their savings account or checking account.

With the money in your brokerage account, you can buy and sell stocks at any time. The broker acts as an intermediary between you and the investment you're interested in purchasing.

Some of the best brokerage firms you can use include;

- E*trade: This trading platform is available both as a web platform and a mobile app. The sleek design, diverse trading tools, and ease of use make it the top preferred brokerage firm. The only drawback with this type of trading platform is the lack of educational materials for investors compared to other platforms.

- TD Ameritrade: This is a beginner-friendly trading platform that offers excellent services to investors. The brokerage firm offers industry-leading stock education to beginner investors and reliable customer services.

  No minimum deposit and has zero stock trade and ETF fee.

- Fidelity: Fidelity is an everyday trading platform with excellent trading tools, and it is optimized for mobile use. It provides a comprehensive retirement plan for investors. A plethora of reading materials on the website makes it an excellent option for beginners who want to take an active role in their investment, including day trading.

- Charles Schwab: Charles Schwab offers excellent financial planning services to investors, and they have excellent stock research options. It is the best for opening IRA accounts, and the presence of the robust tool makes it easy for investors to engage in day trading other trading options.

The only disadvantage to this trading platform is that it doesn't support the streaming of real-time quotes.

- Interactive brokers: Interactive brokers are an institutional-grade and user-friendly desktop trading platform that offer investors access to global markets. They have the lowest commission and lowest margin rates compared to the other platforms. However, it is not ideal for beginners.

- Robinhood: It is an easy-to-use platform that focuses on the basics of stock investment. However, the drawback to this trading platform is the lack of trading tools, phone customer services, and research materials. Their gold membership does include Morningstar reports on select stocks. They do provide both a mobile app and computer web-based trading platform. They do not charge commission fees for any trades, making this an attractive option.

Opening a Robo-advisor account

If you're the kind of investor who doesn't want to use a DIY investment strategy, you can go for a Robo-advisor account and take a passive role in stock investment. Robo-advisors offer investors various investment options such that individual investors don't have to take up as much active work required to carry out an individual investment.

They provide investors a complete investment management approach. Investors only have to state their investment goals, and the Robo-advisors use an algorithm to build an investor's portfolio aimed at achieving the stated goals.

Usually, with Robo-advisor, you only set up the account, pay the management fee, and let the Robo advisor do the rest of the work for you. Most of them generally charge a small percentage (around 0.25%) of your account balance.

For example, Betterment is one of the best Robo advisors for beginner investors because it doesn't require an initial minimum deposit to open the account, and you can start your investment journey with as low as $100 per month.

Step 5: Choose stocks to buy

There are different types of investments you can commit your money to as a beginner. Whether you want to invest in individual stocks or want to use Robo advisors, you have to learn the basic metrics on how to evaluate stocks. Only analyze and select businesses that you already understand. Avoid going for high-volatile stocks until you have experience in stock investment.

You should also learn how to diversify your stocks. When diversifying on your investment portfolio, invest only in companies that you understand. If you're good at evaluating the specific types of stocks, you can have a large segment of those stocks in your portfolio.

If you're looking for easier-to-manage investments, you can go for mutual funds or exchange-traded funds (ETFs). All you need is to open an account with commission-free ETF apps and then decide how much you want to invest.

Mutual funds and ETFs are less risky since they don't require any diversification of your investment portfolio. Instead, they focus on the dollar-cost averaging process that requires you to gradually buy your investment portions rather than buying all the funds at once.

For example, instead of investing $4 000 into a single index fund, you make monthly contributions of about $100.

When starting out, you should start with a single stock before moving to the next stock. Generally, buy at least 100 shares of a single stock at the best pricing, and once comfortable with the investment, repeat the same process until you have a variety of stocks in your portfolio, including mutual funds and ETFs.

Step 6: Set up your budget

If you're new to investing in stocks, you may be wondering;

How much money do you need to start investing in stocks?

When determining the amount you need to buy stocks, you have to consider the market price of each share of stocks. The higher the share price, the more money you need to buy an individual stock unless you're purchasing fractional shares or lower numbers of shares. If you're on a budget, you can go for exchange-traded funds. With as little as $100, you can go for ETFs shares, while mutual funds require a minimum of $1,000.

Additionally, how much you should spend on investing stocks depends on the type of stocks you're buying. If you want to invest through funds, you can make stock funds a large portion of your portfolio which may be wise, especially for long-term investors. For example, if you have 30 years to invest towards your retirement, you can have 80% of your portfolio dedicated to stock funds, and the remaining 20% be dedicated to bonds or individual stocks.

Focus on the long-term investment of your stocks. If you know that an individual stock has the potential for favorable long-term performance, you can focus on having a large segment of this stock in your portfolio. So once you invest in stocks, avoid checking the daily progress of the stocks.

Step 7: Continue investing

The most surefire way to succeed in stocks and grow your money is to continue investing in the best markets. You don't have to do anything extraordinary to obtain extraordinary results!

You can draw your inspiration from Warren Buffet, who is not only a successful long-term investor but also provides the best source of wisdom on stock investment strategies.

The best way to grow your money in stocks is to buy shares at reasonable prices and hold the shares for a long time as long as the business remains great or up to when you need money.

Though you may experience stock volatility along the way, holding the stocks for the long term will produce excellent returns on investment.

Step 8: Manage your stock Portfolio

Tracking daily stock fluctuations is not good for your portfolio health and even your own health. Come up with a way on how to manage your stock portfolio. You can decide to check on your stock investments several times a year to ensure your portfolio is still in line with your stock investment goals.

When approaching your retirement age, you can decide to shift some of your stocks into a fixed-income investment. If your stock portfolio focuses on a specific sector or industry, you try to diversify by buying stocks from a different industry. Ultimately, you should pay more attention to geographical diversification.

Further, depending on your risk tolerance and age, you can consider building your portfolio by investing in international funds, bonds, and income funds. You can also consider investing in high dividend stocks and other growth stocks.

Chapter Summary

The earlier you start investing in stocks, and the longer you hold your money in the investment, the more you grow your money. Investing your money for retirement while in your 30's will result in higher returns on investment after you retire.

If you have basic knowledge of stock investment, you can follow the above step and watch your money grow. Investment is a process, and you keep on learning and experimenting to obtain the best.

In the next chapter, you will learn how to invest through ETFs.

Chapter Three

Passive investment through ETFs

An increasing number of investors are using Exchange-traded funds (ETFs) to diversify their portfolios and ease the trading process.

ETFs are an investment basket that consists of different securities, commodities, bonds, mutual funds, and foreign currency funds traded in a stock exchange. A single ETF share can allow you to easily track the performance of hundreds or even thousands of companies listed on the stock market. It combines both features and benefits of stocks, bonds, and mutual funds. Just like stocks, ETFs are traded throughout a trading day based on demand and supply and trade at market-determined prices.

Unlike stocks which allow you to invest in a single company, an ETF allows you to invest in a basket of companies providing you with the diversification needed to reduce your risk exposure. The ticker symbols used during the exchange allow you to track the prices of the ETF shares.

You can easily buy and sell these securities in the secondary market like you would any other stocks. There is no need to buy individual components of these securities. They often have lower transaction fees compared to other types of funds.

How do ETFs work?

The provider of the ETF owns the securities and comes up with an index that tracks the performance of the ETF shares and then sells them to the investors. The shareholders only own a portion of the ETF shares but do not have ownership of the underlying securities in the fund.

Though they do not actually own the funds but have the right to indirectly claim a portion of the returns and residual value during liquidation of the funds. ETFs do also pay dividends as well.

Just like other types of stocks, ETFs are listed in the stock market and they can be traded during normal trading hours. Passively managed ETFs are also associated with very low annual fees that go to the firm's analysts and managers, making them much more profitable.

Best S&P 500 ETFs

An S&P 500 ETF is one of the inexpensive and diversified means of gaining exposure to US stocks. According to Warren Buffet, you should focus on investing in a low-cost S&P 500 index fund.

His reasoning is that; it is difficult to create a portfolio that outperforms the US S&P 500 index in the long term. The index delivers an average annual rate of return of 10% for a period of over 90 years.

In addition, buying shares of S&P 500 ETF is a great way for the investors to have a slice of the market at a small price. There are three major ETFs for tracking the S&P 500 performance.

They include; SPY, IVV, and VOO. These are among the S&P 500 exchange-traded funds with the lowest fees. In addition, the SPY has the highest liquidity.

SPY ETF

The SPY ETF, also known as the **SPDR S&P 500 ETF,** is one of the most popular funds that tracks 500 mid-cap and largest companies in the US stocks. The top 10 companies listed in the stock index include heavily weighted technology-related companies.

Most of the funds are allocated into common stocks included in the S&P 500 index. They also have better returns than the average return of other S&P index funds.

IVV ETF

It is also known as the **iShares Core S&P 500 ETF,** which has the highest trading price. It tracks investment results from index funds that have the largest US capitalization.

IVV ETF investment is suitable for those who want to diversify the investment portfolio by seeking long-term growth opportunities.

The price affects how many shares of the funds to buy. For example, you can buy 21 shares of IVV ETF, while a similar amount can buy 23 shares of VOO-ETF.

Both funds track the same index, but they generate different returns and yields. According to a report from Morningstar, IVV ETF provides the highest yield for a period of 12 months. The returns are from the interests received and dividends. While VOO ETF reports the highest price return (financial gains from the ETF investment) for a period of 5 years.

VOO ETF

The VOO ETF or the **Vanguard S&P 500 ETF** is a great way for investors to gain profits from the stock market, and at the same time, it limits the downside risks associated with these index funds.

It has the lowest management fee compared to other S&P 500 ETF for tracking performance, and it is highly liquid with an increasing daily trading volume.

If you have low-risk tolerance and want to initiate a long-term trading strategy, you can go for VOO ETF. Investors can gain from the annual dividend yield, and it carries an expense ratio of about 0.03%.

Therefore, choosing the best fund for your portfolio is an individual decision. You can consider factors such as the returns, expense ratio, trading costs, and the price of the funds before making your decision.

Types of ETFs

There are different types of ETFs, with each having varying levels of risks. They don't offer a one-size-fits-all solution. Therefore, you have to evaluate the benefits of each type of fund, including the management costs, quality of investment, and how easily you can buy and sell the exchange-traded funds.

They include;

Diversified passive ETFs: Passively managed funds mimic the performance of the common stock market indexes such as the S&P 500 and the Dow Jones Industrial Average (DJIA), among others. The major ETF indexes closely follow this performance benchmark to evaluate market performance.

Niche Passive ETFs: These mimic ETF's shares from a small sector of S&P 500 or smaller companies listed in the Russell 2000. A niche passive ETF ensures investors are able to fine-tune their investment portfolio strategies.

Active ETFs: In this type of fund, investors don't rely on the index benchmark. Instead they focus on their own judgment when choosing an investment.

Compared to passive ETFs, active ETFs have a higher potential to outperform the market benchmark resulting in a higher portfolio turnover rate. It also carries a higher risk and high costs.

Stock ETFs: This type of ETF holds specific equity or stock portfolios. Stock ETFs are treated similarly to stocks since you can buy and sell them for a profit. You can also trade them via the stock exchange throughout the trading day.

Index ETFs: They imitate a particular stock index like the S&P 500 index. Index ETFs track particular classes of stocks, foreign markets, and emerging equity markets. Index ETFs can track the values of the Dow Jones Industrial Average, S&P 500, Nasdaq 100, and Russell 200 indexes. For example, the Invesco QQQ ETF tracks the performance of the top 100 performing companies listed on the Nasdaq exchange, also known as the Nasdaq-100 index.

Bond ETFs: Bond ETFs are specifically for investors who want to invest in bonds and fixed-income securities. Investors can focus on a specific type of bond or diversify their portfolio with bonds of different types and maturity dates.

Commodity ETFs: This type of ETF allows you to invest in companies related to physical commodities like natural resources or agricultural products. Investors can hold both investments in physical commodities and equity-related investments. For example, you can own a bar of physical gold and at the same time own stock shares in a company that mines gold.

International ETFs: Investors who want to invest in a currency or basket of currencies, including the foreign exchange market, use this form of currency ETF. These ETFs track various international currencies like the US dollar, Canadian dollar, British Pound, Euro, and Japanese Yen.

Pros and cons of ETFs

Pros

1. **Tax efficiency:** One of the major advantages of exchange-traded funds over mutual funds is tax efficiency. ETFs can reduce portfolio turnover, making investors avoid short-term gains that lead to increased tax rates.

2. **Lower expense ratios:** Compared to mutual funds and other securities, ETFs have a low transaction fee and costs. Exchange-traded funds place the costs of operation on the brokers or the exchange resulting in a lower expense ratio. While a mutual fund will bear all the costs.

3. **Transparency:** ETF operates in a more transparent manner compared to mutual funds and hedge funds. ETFs usually have daily reporting on the fund's holdings. As a result, investors are aware of the daily performance of their funds and are able to come up with better ways to manage risks.

4. **Diversification:** Exchange-traded funds allow investors to diversify their investment. Though it might take you long to acquire all the components in a particular basket, ETFs deliver all these benefits into your portfolio with just a click of a button.

5. **No minimum investment:** Unlike mutual funds that require you to start with minimum investment, ETFs don't have any

minimum requirements. You can buy a few shares of the ETF as desired.

Cons

1. **Transaction costs:** Since exchange-traded funds are traded in an exchange, you have to pay for the brokerage commission fee. This can increase your expense ratio.

2. **Liquidity issues:** When dealing with other types of securities, you will be aware of the changes in the current market prices before selling your shares. Some ETFs are not traded as often thus may be harder to unload or sell on short notice.

3. **Distribution of capital gains:** Sometimes ETF investments may result in distributed taxable gains since managers have to buy and sell stocks in order to match the specified benchmark.

   For instance, if you buy government ETF bonds, you have to pay federal income tax. Further, some ETFs are more volatile than others. Therefore, you should determine the risks associated with different ETFs before making your investment decisions.

4. **Trading flexibility:** The flexibility of ETF trading encourages buying and selling of funds at the wrong times.

Best ETF trading strategies

Exchanged-traded funds are great investments for beginners because of their various benefits, low-risk, low costs, and associated diversification. Its features also make it a great trading and investment strategy for new investors and traders. Some of these strategies include;

1. Dollar-cost averaging

This strategy requires investors to regularly buy the assets at a fixed-dollar amount regardless of the changes in the cost of the assets. New investors with a stable income can invest a couple of dollars each month in an ETF instead of saving the money in a low-interest saving account. By investing a set amount over periodic purchases, you're able to average out the average share price and reduce the impact of overall market volatility.

2. Asset allocation

It requires you to allocate different categories of assets to a portion of your portfolio. You can invest in securities like stocks, bonds, and commodities as a way to diversify your portfolio.

The low cost of ETFs makes it easy for investors to implement asset allocation and diversify their investment. For example, investors in the early 20s can invest 100% of the money on equity ETFs, and as they get older, they can shift their investment and become less aggressive. They can decide to invest 55% in bond ETFs and about 45% in equity ETFs.

3. Swing trading

Swing trades are types of trade that take advantage of changes in stocks or other securities like commodities and currencies. The concept of swing trading is basically opening set positions you plan to hold for days, weeks, or even months at a time and selling for a profit. This is contrary to day trading, which involves buying and selling securities over a period of seconds, minutes, or hours, but always closing your positions by market close.

4. Sector rotation

Beginner investors can easily implement sector rotation ETF strategy based on the specific stages of the economic life cycle. Basically, you can constantly buy into the sectors of the economy that are making the highest gains during that period of time. There are different classes of ETFs and a wide range of sectors, making it easy for new investors to choose to trade in a particular asset class or sector that they have knowledge of.

For example, if you're knowledgeable on technology and looking for high-growth potential, you can invest in technology-related ETFs such as the Invesco QQQ ETF and track the Nasdaq-100 index. If you're interested in the commodity market, you can trade in commodity ETF like the Invesco DB commodity index tracking fund (DBC).

Another example, if you want to invest in the biotechnology sector, you can do so through the iShares Nasdaq Biotechnology ETF (IBB).

Alternatively, you can choose consumer staples through the Consumer Staples Select Sector SPDR Fund. This is perfect if you're more risk-averse and want to invest in a historically more defensive sector that tends to weather periods of economic downturn but may also have less growth potential.

5. *Hedging*

Beginner investors sometimes have to use a hedging strategy as a way to protect against risks associated with their investment portfolio.

For example, concerns about the risks associated with the US blue chips equities have led to the use of put options. The concepts of options trading strategies are a bit beyond the scope of this book.However, if you initiate a put option, you pay a premium to begin your position and will make an exponential return as the price of shares drop. Some investors that open large positions in an ETF will also pay a much smaller premium to purchase put options in case the stock crashes to offset their losses. This is the concept of hedging.

Factors to consider when selecting an ETF

There are over 1000 exchange-traded funds in the market, which can make it difficult to choose the best ETF for your portfolio. The quickest way to narrow your selection is to focus on the fund's information that enables you to match your investment objectives with the right ETF.

To pick the right ETF, you have to consider the following factors;

1. *Level of assets*

A good exchange-traded fund should have a minimum level of assets, with the least threshold being $10 million. Any ETF with a threshold below this will have few investors interested in the fund.

2. Trading activity

Another factor you have to consider is whether there is sufficient trading volume for the ETF you want to buy. There are ETFs that trade almost millions of shares on a daily basis while others don't trade at all.

Trading volume is a great indicator of ETF liquidity no matter the asset class. If there is a high trading volume, the more liquid the funds and a tighter bid offer.

3. Asset class

The asset class or an underlying index is an important factor when selecting the exchange-traded funds. If you're looking for diversification of your portfolio, you should select ETFs that have a widely followed index instead of choosing those with an uncertain index or ETF from a narrow industry.

4. Tracking errors

Most of the ETFs closely track the underlying indexes, while others don't closely monitor them. These ETFs can record a certain degree of tracking errors. Investors always prefer ETFs with a lower tracking error over those with a greater degree of tracking error.

5. Costs

Though ETFs are cost-effective, you have to weigh other related costs such as commissions and fees. Compare the cost of investment while trading with different indexes and mutual funds.

Some ETFs do charge management fees, and if you're actively trading, you have to consider the commission you have to pay and any other related costs associated with that exchange-traded fund.

How to invest in ETFs

It is important to note that ETFs vary depending on the fund's demand, complexity, costs, and issuer. Exchange-traded funds have costs that vary from one fund to the next, even those that track the same index.

How to invest in any of these funds is largely dependent on one's preferences. For investors who prefer a hands-on approach, investing in ETFs is much easier. Most of these online brokers offer standard access to the assets. Though the ETF cost is very low, the transaction fee and other related costs vary by broker.

On the other hand, Robo-advisors create a portfolio from low-cost ETFs and give investors access to the assets.

You also have to choose your asset class. That is, do you want to invest in stocks, bonds, mutual funds, or commodities? Come up with the percentage you're going to allocate to each class of asset to your portfolio.

Your next step is diversification of your investment strategy. You can decide to focus your investment in a specific market segment or building your wealth across a wider class of assets. For example, investing in a specific industry like renewable energy in an individual country or investing in an ETF that holds international assets.

Once you choose the type of investment to focus on, your next step is to select the index you will track with your ETF. A good index should be able to cover the larger part of the market you want to follow.

If a particular index concentrates on a particular industry or country, the riskier it will be compared to indexes that track a wider market. Further, you have to select the right index to track your ETFs equities.

Chapter Summary

Exchange-traded funds (ETFs) are one of the best stock investment strategies for beginners. It is cost-effective and provides you with a great way to diversify your portfolio through its basket of securities.

ETF gives you an option to invest in equities, bonds, mutual funds, currencies, and commodities. All these securities are traded in the stock exchange market throughout a trading day. There are different types of ETFs, and you can select the right fund for your portfolio based on your investment goals. There are also different trading strategies you can choose based on your investment portfolio.

In the next chapter, you will learn how to create passive income through investing in dividends.

Chapter Four

How To Create Passive Income Through Dividend Investing

Stock investments are one of the greatest means by which individuals can generate passive income. This is because stock investments distribute some returns in the form of dividend payments. The dividends which are paid can form a stream of passive income which individuals can live off of.

One of the common strategies income investors use is creating a portfolio with high-paying dividend stocks. For example, the ETF that trades under the symbol DVY uses this exact strategy. DVY contains high dividend-paying equities contained within the Dow Jones Industrial Average to produce significant regular dividend payments.

Generating passive income is the ultimate goal for every investor. The money you invest will earn you more money, allowing you to live a comfortable life after retirement.

The success of building your investment portfolio depends on the amount of passive income you can create from dividends and interest during harsh economic periods. Continuous research and monitoring of your investment position are very important to achieve this.

What are dividends?

A dividend is a regular payment in the form of profits to investors who own shares in a company's stock. It is the greatest way for investors to earn returns from their investments in stocks.

Not all companies pay dividends, so if you're looking forward to receiving dividends from your investment, you should select dividend paying stocks. Dividend stocks provide a stable stream of income, especially if you invest in a company that increases dividend payout every year.

High-growth companies like biotech and other tech companies usually reinvest their profits back into the company to expand them; thus they don't pay dividends to the investors.

Investors rely on dividends to determine the company's financial stability and well-being. If they think the value of dividends will reduce, they devalue the stock, and as a result, the price of shares reduces.

For example, companies like Apple, American Electric Power, CVS, Disney, Principal Financial Group, and Target pay dividends to their shareholders.

Types of dividends

Different companies use different types of dividends to pay out their shareholders. They include;

Cash dividends: Most of the companies pay their shareholders in cash. The payout is sent directly to the shareholder's brokerage account.

Stock dividends: In this type of dividend, instead of paying cash to the shareholders, the company pays the shareholders with additional shares of the company's stock.

Preferred dividends: This is the dividend paid to shareholders who own preferred stock. Preferred stock usually has a fixed payment of dividends, unlike common stocks, dividends paid on a quarterly basis.

Special dividends: Some companies accumulate the dividends for several years and distribute the profits to the shareholders. Therefore, special dividends are not paid on a regular basis like other common stocks.

Dividend reinvestment programs (DRIPs): This is another strategy that allows DRIPs investors to reinvest the dividends back into the company's stock.

How often do companies pay dividends?

Most companies pay dividends on a quarterly basis though there are a few that pay on a monthly basis or even semi-annually. Before the payment of the dividend, the board of directors must approve them.

The company also has to announce when to pay the dividends to shareholders, how much to pay per share of stock, and the ex-dividend date.

For the investors to receive the dividends, they must own the shares of stock by the ex-dividend date. If the stock shares are bought after the ex-dividend date, then they will not be eligible for dividend payment. Investors who sell their stock shares after the ex-dividend date also have a right to receive dividends because they owned the shares.

How to evaluate a company's dividends?

There are various methods you can use to learn about the company's dividends and compare the price per share with that of similar companies. The commonly used methods include;

Dividend per share (DPS)

Investors usually search for companies that increase dividend payments each year. The dividend per share method enables investors to know the amount distributed per share of stock during a certain period of time.

Tracking the dividend price per share enables you to know the companies that will be able to grow your passive income over time.

For example, if you own 20 shares and the company pays $2 per year as cash dividends, then you will receive $40 per year in dividends.

Dividend Yield

Online brokerage platforms and financial websites usually report the dividend yield to investors. Dividend yield measures the company's annual dividends divided by the price of stocks on a specific date.

For example, if you bought Apple stocks at $60 per share and pays dividends of $0.45 on a quarterly basis, then the annual dividends will be $0.45*4 is $1.80. To calculate the dividend yield, take the annual dividend of $1.80 and divide by the price per share of stock ($60): $1.80/$60 is 0.03 or 3%. 3% is the stock's "dividend yield."

Dividend yield and stock prices work hand-in-hand. If the price of one goes up, then the other often goes down. Any successful company should be able to increase dividends each year. Let's assume our Apple Company mentioned above increases the dividend by 7.2% per year. Your annual dividend will also increase from $1.80 to $3.60, which is double the original payment amount after a period of time. Your dividend yield will also double to 6% ($3.60/$60). The longer you hold your shares of stock, the higher the dividend yield.

The stock dividend yield can go up when;

The company increases its dividend payout. If you buy the stock at $100 per share and the dividend payout is $4, an increase of the company's dividend by 10% will increase the annual dividend payout to $4.40 per share. Assuming the stock price remains the same, then the dividend yield will be 4.4%.

· The stock prices reduce while the dividend remains the same. When the stock price reduces to $90 per share, and the dividend remains the same at $4, the yield will be more than 4.4%.

It is important to analyze any dividend yield of above 4% as it is a clear indication that you will have an unsustainable dividend payout. However, there exist exceptions to the 4% rule, especially if you bought stocks that pay dividends, such as real estate investment trusts.

How to build your dividend portfolio to increase the income stream

If you want to build your dividend portfolio, you should start with small portions of stock and continue scaling up over time. You can start by opening a brokerage account that has a low commission fee, such as Robinhood, and start trading.

Having an account with a platform that charges a low commission is the key to reducing unnecessary spending in sunk costs paid to brokerage firms. Low or even commission-free trading from a brokerage saves you a lot of money which maximizes your returns.

Take advantage of the various options provided to mitigate the investment risks in your portfolio. Even during low economic periods with a downside trend, you can initiate a hedging strategy to boost your monthly income from the dividends payments.

Further, you can follow the dividend allocation strategy in your portfolio by allocating different types of dividends to diversify your portfolio.

For example;

· Allocating 45% of your portfolio to Dividend Aristocrats

· Allocating 20% of your portfolio to Dividend Kings

· Allocating 25% of your dividend portfolio to upcoming dividend stocks. This includes stocks that have shown a high growth rate with an increased track record of dividends over a period of time. These stocks provide rewarding benefits to the shareholders though they cannot be classified as dividend growth stocks like the above dividend Aristocrats and dividend king.

·Allocating the remaining 10% of your portfolio to international dividend growth stocks. You can invest in global growth dividend funds or international blue-chip dividend growth stocks.

Dividend Aristocrats

These dividend growth funds demonstrate an excellent track record of success, followed by dividend kings. Dividend Aristocrats is a group of 65 S&P 500 stocks that have demonstrated a dividend increase for over 25 years. The stocks also have a history of outperforming the market.

For a company to be classified as a Dividend Aristocrat it should;

·Be included in the S&P 500 index

·Have demonstrated a consecutive increase in dividends for over 25 years

·Meet minimum liquidity requirements and size.

Dividend Aristocrats firms are more reliable, and investors can receive a reliable source of income. These companies are also industry leaders with an impressive annual return even during the recession, and they're less affected.

How to compound your wealth using the snowball effect

The key to building a successful stream of income is to gradually increase your investment portfolio. You can start your investment with small amounts and take advantage of the power of compounding to grow your income.

The power compounding is associated with the snowball effect in which small actions taken over time can result in big results. Just like a snowball moves down the hill, it picks up more snow forming a giant ball as it reaches the bottom.

Investors can also use the snowball effect to grow their wealth. Start by investing in high-quality dividend stocks to generate higher dividends returns. The longer you invest in the stocks, the higher the returns.

Typically, your original stocks investments return in your earnings, and time helps you harness the power of compounding and maximize your wealth. The compounding interest is not a get-rich-quick strategy, and it takes a lot of time before you can realize the capital gains.

For example, Warren Buffet's wealth is over $80 billion, and most of his wealth is from taking advantage of snowball effects over a period of time. He compounded his wealth through investing in;

- Investor friendly businesses

- Stocks with a strong competitive advantage

- Trades with fair prices.

The rule of thumb is to pick good stocks at the right times and sticking with them as long as they give you good returns. You can also build your wealth through investing in the same business or diversifying your portfolio.

Chapter Summary

Investing in stocks is a great way of building your passive income. If you want to increase your income stream, you can build a diversified investment portfolio with different asset classes.

Once you select stocks to invest in, you only need to monitor your investment and watch your money grow. The longer you hold stocks in a company, the more returns in dividends you receive from the company's earnings.

In the next chapter, you will learn stock investment strategies; Warren Buffet, the value investing strategy, and price-to-earnings ratio.

Chapter Five

Warren Buffett, Value Investing, & P/E Ratios

There are different ways you can invest in stocks, but most of them fall into three basic categories: Value investing strategies, growth investing strategies, and index investing strategies.

All these stock investment strategies are influenced by an investor's mindset and the strategies they take to build their passive income. For most investors, financial status, investment goals, and risk tolerance are the major contributors to the type of strategy to choose.

Most investors prefer low-cost stock investments, reinvesting dividends, or going for diversified index funds to build their wealth. However, experienced investors prefer to engage in individual stocks and gradually build their portfolios step-by-step based on the analysis of the individual companies.

Those who like the do-it-yourself strategy, like the father of value investing Benjamin Graham together with Warren Buffett, use financial analysis to invest in stocks that provide better returns than your average stock returns.

Graham came up with a lot of standards and principles that modern investors still follow. Warren Buffet follows the Benjamin Graham School of value investing, which is a widely used investment philosophy across the world.

This investment strategy enables one to amass a huge fortune from stock investing. The idea here is to play a long-term game because the strategy focuses on buying businesses and not just stocks.

That means the investor should be looking at the big picture and not the temporary performance of stocks. Warren Buffet is one of the world's most known billionaire value investors who does his homework before choosing the industry he invests in. And when he is ready, he gets into the market and stays there for a long time.

Value Investing Strategy

This is an investment strategy that allows you to invest in undervalued stocks. These stocks usually trade at a lower price than their intrinsic value or the book value.

In the stock market, undervalued stock shares mean having cheap and discounted stocks. Successful investors look for undervalued stocks (valuable stocks that are not widely recognized), buy them at a discount and hold them for the long term. These discounted shares earn them a lot of profits.

Value investors buy securities at unjustifiably low prices based on the intrinsic worth of the stock. However, there is no universally recognized method to measure the intrinsic measure. Investors rely on the company's fundamentals such as financial performance, cash flow statements, revenue, company's earnings, and profits to determine its worth.

Other factors that can determine the intrinsic value of stocks include the company's brand, target market, business model, and competitive advantage.

Buffet follows the value investing strategy to determine the market value and grow his investment. He doesn't rely on the rule of demand and supply when trading in the stock market. According to his famous paraphrase of the Benjamin Graham quote, "A market is a voting machine in the short run but a weighing machine in the long run."

He analyzes the company as a whole and buys stocks based on the overall potential for the company's growth. His ultimate goal is on the ownership of securities in a company that can generate more earnings in the future. Therefore, he doesn't seek capital gains but holds the stocks for the long term.

When he invests in a company's stocks, he is more interested in how the said company will make money as a business. He isn't interested in how the market will recognize the worthiness of the company.

What to look for when using the Buffet investment approach

To identify valued low-priced stocks, you have to consider the following factors;

1. Company's performance

Typically, return on equity (ROE) or return on investment (ROI) is the rate at which shareholders receive income from the shares invested. Investors use ROE to determine whether the company is consistent with its performance and compare it with that of companies in the same industry.

To get better results on the performance of the company you should analyze the historical performance for the past 5 to 10 years.

ROE= Net income/Shareholders equity

2. Company debts

Another factor you have to consider is the debt-to-equity (D/E) ratio. Maintaining a small amount of debt ensures you generate more earnings from the shareholder's equity instead of borrowed money.

D/E ratio= Total liabilities/Shareholder's equity

The ratio serves as a way for investors to analyze how the company finances its assets, and its equity should be proportioned to the debts. A higher ratio means higher debts are financing the company.

A higher ratio results in increased interest expense and volatile earnings. To avoid this, investors prefer to use long-term debts to calculate the debt ratio instead of using total liabilities.

3. Company's profits margins

The profitability of a company not only depends on its profit margins but also on being able to consistently increase its profits. Investors should look at the historical profit margins for at least 5 years to get accurate profitability of the company.

$$Profit\ margin = Net\ income/Net\ sales$$

If the company has a higher profit margin, it means the company has efficient management, and it is able to control its expenses.

4. Is it a public company?

Value investing requires you to go for companies that have been in existence for several years because they have stood the test of time even though they're currently undervalued.

Buffet only considers companies that have been in existence for 10 years after their first initial public offering (IPO). A company's historical performance demonstrates its ability or inability to add value to the shareholder. Keep in mind that the historical performance isn't a guarantee of the future performance of the company.

Therefore, you should determine how the company will continue performing as it did in the past. Securities and Exchange Commission (SEC) requires all public companies to regularly publish their financial statements. You can use this information to analyze the company's past and present performance.

5. Company's value

How cheap is the company you want to invest in? To determine this, you have to look at the intrinsic value of the company by looking at factors such as the company's assets, earnings, and revenue.

Typically, the intrinsic value of the company is always higher than its liquidation value. This is because the liquidation value doesn't include the company's brand name, among other intangibles.

According to Buffet, you have to determine the company's intrinsic value as a whole and then compare it with the current market capitalization. Coming up with accurate intrinsic value provides you with the total worth of the company.

Price-to-earnings (P/E) ratio

The price-to-earnings (P/E) ratio is one of the widely used metrics to measure a Company's performance. It helps investors and analysts know the market value of the stocks in relation to the company's earnings. This is a good indicator of whether a particular stock is a good investment or not.

It also helps determine the future stock price, whether the prices are going to rise or drop, and how the prices compare with other market peers in the same industry.

A high ratio is an indicator that the stock prices are high relative to its earnings and probably they're undervalued. Conversely, if the P/E ratio is low, it indicates a low price of stocks in relation to their earnings.

High growth companies like those in the technology industry have higher P/E ratios. And due to its potential for future growth, investors are ready to pay the higher price to acquire the shares.

P/E ratio is easy to calculate, and it is given by the company's stock prices divided by earnings per share (EPS).

P/E ratio= Price per share/earnings per share

In other words, if the company's earnings per share are $3 and selling stocks at $30 per share, then the P/E ratio will be $10 ($30/$3=$10).

The P/E ratio can also determine the future earnings of the company. If the company expects the earnings to rise, the company may increase its dividend payouts to the shareholders. Again higher earnings followed by increased dividends will result in higher stock prices.

Further, you can easily calculate the stock earnings yield by inverting the P/E ratio.

Stock yield=Earnings per share/ Price per share

This enables you to easily analyze returns you're earning from the company proceeds and compare them with other forms of investments such as bonds, treasury bills, currency, real estate, and more.

Chapter Summary

Investing in stocks based on the company's intrinsic value provides you with the potential growth of your investment. Value investing is one of the greatest strategies that help investors to go for underestimated stocks, buy them at a discount, and make lots of profit. According to Warren Buffet, there are various strategies you have to follow and get the best out of the value investing strategy.

Always do due diligence before buying stocks. Do not buy stocks because they have an attractive P/E ratio, do your research to know how good they are as well as the underlying historical performance of the company.

In the next chapter, you will learn about the growth investing strategy.

Chapter Six

Growth Investing Strategy

People have different opinions and styles when it comes to money management but getting money working for you is the ultimate goal for all investing strategies. When and how you achieve financial independence depends on some factors, such as your personal risk tolerance and time.

However, there are different investment strategies and principles that investors can use to grow their income. No matter the approach you use, your goal is to grow your investment and increase your earnings.

What is growth investing?

Growth investing is another stock investment strategy where you invest in high growth stocks, which are typically small or young emerging companies that are expected to grow at an above average rate compared to the market as a whole or to other companies within that sector. A lot of these companies tend to be those with new, disruptive and innovative technologies that have the potential to fundamentally change the market they're in.

In this type of strategy, instead of going for undervalued or low-cost stocks, you can go for investments that have the potential for higher earnings in the future. To succeed in this type of investment, you have to evaluate the current health of the stock you want to invest in and its growth potential.

You should always look at the future prospects of the industry you want to thrive in. For example, what is the future of AI, and how will it affect the technology company you want to invest in?

Before investing in any company, there must be evidence showing that the company is going to grow. You can get this information by looking at the company's historical performance report. In other words, any growth stock company should be growing. It should be able to show a consistent trend on the earnings and revenues.

Unlike value investing, investors following growth investing focus on small or young companies that have already demonstrated potential for future growth, such as companies in the technology industry. These companies do not pay dividends to the shareholders because they need capital to sustain their expansion by reinvesting that money into their company.

Growth investors continuously look for investments in individual stocks, mutual funds, and exchange-traded funds that have the potential for generating higher profits. The investment you make should also align with your short-term or long-term financial goals and your risk tolerance.

Growth in the company's earnings or generated revenue is usually reflected in increased share price. Growth investors may buy stocks at a price higher than the company's intrinsic value because they believe that the high growth rate will boost the intrinsic value of the company to higher levels.

Investors rely on financial metrics such as earning-per-share (EPS), return on equity (ROE), share price performance, and profit margin to determine the company's worth.

How to fully utilize growth investing strategy

Step 1. Prepare your finances

As a rule, you shouldn't buy stocks with money you might need within the next 5 years. That's because the market prices can rise over the long term, it can also drop without any warnings. Therefore, do not put yourself in a position that forces you to sell your stocks during low periods. Instead, you should focus on buying the stocks when other investors are selling them.

Step 2. Focus on the growth prospects

Now that your stock investment is giving you a lot of finances, it's high time to arm yourself with more knowledge on how to build more wealth. You can also decide to invest in well-established businesses that have a history of producing positive earnings.

Alternatively, you can rely on quantitative metrics that measure return on the invested capital, the operating margin, and the compounding of the annual growth of the company. Growth investors only buy from the best performing businesses that demonstrate consistent market gains.

It is also important to focus on buying stocks from the companies and industries that you already know. If you have knowledge in the marketing industry or cloud software services, you can use this knowledge to evaluate the performance of the industries and choose the best business for your investment. This strategy ensures you don't chase returns by jumping from one industry to the next since it's working better at that moment.

Step 3. Stock selection

Now that you have identified where to buy the stocks, it is now time to begin your investment journey. This requires you to decide how much cash you intend to set aside for the growth investment strategy.

If you're a beginner, it is good to start small, like allocating 10% of your portfolio funds towards growth investment. As you gain more experience by investing in different types of markets as well as understanding the volatility of the stock market, you can increase this ratio.

There is a high risk involved when making your decision on which industry to invest in because the growth stock market is very aggressive and volatile. For this reason, a long-term horizon is the most preferred approach since it offers more flexibility to adjust your portfolio towards this style of investment.

If you're too anxious with your portfolio, it means you have set a high allocation of funds towards the growth stocks. But if you're worried about making losses or about a drop in stocks in the past, then you can focus your investment on more diverse options instead of investing in individual growth stocks.

Buying Growth Funds

The best way to get exposure to a range of growth-focused stock options is through a fund. For example, most of the retirement plans feature a diverse range of growth stock options forming the basis of your stock investment strategies.

You can decide to buy a low-cost growth-based index fund to diversify your portfolio instead of buying mutual funds. That's because investment managers who run the mutual funds try to outperform the market, while index funds rely on computer algorithms to help match the stock returns with those of the industry benchmark.

Screening growth stocks

If you like-do-it-yourself investment strategy, you can decide to buy individual stocks. This step provides you with the potential for gaining higher market returns, but it is associated with higher risks than when investing in a diversified fund.

Investors should screen for growth stock factors such as;

- Earnings per share should be above average growth or above profits the company makes each year.

- An above-average gross margin or profitability. This is the percentage of sales that is converted into profits.

- Demonstrated high historical growth in terms of revenue and sales.

- High return on investment. This is a great way to measure how the company efficiently spends its cash.

You should also screen for risks associated with your investment. For example, if the company has a low market capitalization, it will face a lot of competition and other disruptions that threaten the existence of the entire business.

Again, if the company has recorded an annual loss in the past 3 years, then it is not ideal for a growth investor.

Another factor you have to look at is the change in the management, especially the CEO position. Poor management of the firm results in low operating metrics, and this affects the profitability of the company.

Step 4: Maximize your returns

Although the stock market is very volatile, you should hold each of your investments for a couple of years to maximize your returns. You should also keep an eye on price changes and adjust your portfolio accordingly.

Some of the reasons why you have to watch the price changes include;

- If a particular stock has gained more value and makes a higher percentage of your portfolio. In such cases, it is good to rebalance your portfolio by minimizing your exposure to that portion of the stock.

- If the stock price increases above your estimated value, you can consider selling it and use the funds to invest in other reasonable priced stocks.

There are a lot of reasons you may decide to sell your stocks and adjust your portfolio. But if you did thorough homework before purchasing a particular type of stock, your job will mostly be sitting patiently and watching as the power of compounding returns grows your wealth in the next 10, 20, or more years.

Types of growth investments stocks

There are different categories of assets that have shown a higher potential for growth. They include;

1. Small-cap stocks

The market capitalization or the company's net worth is ideal for measuring the company's size. While there is no universal determinant of whether a company is a small-cap, a micro-cap, medium-cap, or large-cap, analysts classify companies with $300 million to $2 billion capitalizations as small-cap.

Small-cap companies are still in the initial stages of development, and there is a high potential for appreciation of stock prices. Most of the small-cap stocks have historically demonstrated high returns compared to stocks from blue-chip companies.

The volatile nature of small-cap stocks represents a high degree of risks, and they tend to outperform large-cap stocks during recovery periods.

2. Technology and healthcare stocks

Innovative companies in the healthcare and technology-related industries are an excellent choice for growth investors. The stock prices of these companies increase rapidly within a very short period of time.

For example, the stocks of the Roku Streaming Media Company surged a few months after its initial public offering (IPO).

3. Speculative investments

Aggressive investors and speculators tend to invest in high-risk growth securities such as foreign currency, penny stocks, real estate, and options contracts. Picking the right type of high-risk growth instrument will result in high returns. But you should also be very careful with these financial instruments because you can lose every cent of your principal amount.

Chapter Summary

Growth investment is one of the greatest ways for investors to grow their money through short-term and long-term capital appreciation processes. Growth companies have higher growth potential as compared to value investing.

When evaluating growth investments, you should look for factors such as the rate of growth, the amount of capital to invest, and the type of risk involved. There are also other elements that play an important role in how much returns investors get from their investment.

If you want to be a growth investor, you should examine your return on equity (ROE), increasing earnings per share (EPS), and the projected earnings of the company.

In the next chapter, you will learn how to build your investment portfolio.

Chapter Seven

Building Your Portfolio

B uilding your investment portfolio doesn't have to be a complicated affair. Individual investors who want to invest in stocks fall into two groups. One group is interested in purchasing a particular type of stock but has little knowledge on how to capture the performance of the entire asset class.

While the second group goes for managed investments such as stocks, mutual funds, exchange-traded funds, index funds, or even go for privately managed accounts. This gives you a good chance to capture all the performance features of the asset class.

No matter what kind of investor you want to be, you can easily build a simple and cost-effective portfolio using funds or rely on the services of Robo-advisors.

Your investment portfolio should include different types of assets under one roof. These assets include stocks, mutual funds, exchange-traded funds, bonds, and currencies. Assuming you have a taxable brokerage account, 401(K) account, and an individual retirement account, you have to analyze each of these accounts before deciding on how to invest in them.

If you want to be passively involved with your portfolio, you can seek the services of Robo-advisors or hire a financial advisor to manage the assets on your behalf. In this topic, you will learn the simple ways you can create your investment portfolio.

How to build your portfolio

Step 1: Establish your investment benchmark

The first step of coming up with a good investment portfolio is to come up with your investment goals that will act as the benchmark to measure the performance of your portfolio. A well-established benchmark helps you compare your investment outcome to know whether you're working towards achieving the performance characteristic of the particular asset class.

For example, you can create a portfolio that captures the small-cap, mid-cap, and large-cap stocks in the S&P 500 Index. You can use published financial statements on the company's performance to structure your portfolio as well as compare the performance of different company stocks.

The S&P index classifies stocks into 10 broad categories with several subclasses. You can rely on this information to find the percentage market weighting of each category in the stock index. This is an excellent guide for the diversification of your portfolio.

In addition to setting up your financial goals, you have to consider your age, how long it will take you to grow your investment, the amount of capital needed to buy the stocks, and analyze your future income needs.

A 25-year-old beginning his professional career requires a different investment strategy than a 45-year-old married person who has to pay for the child's education and save for retirement.

Step 2: Personality and risk tolerance

One important factor to consider when creating your portfolio is your risk tolerance and personality. In other words, the amount of investment losses you can accept in exchange for earning a return on investment.

Your risk tolerance is not only associated with how long you have to wait before you can achieve your financial goals but also whether you're mentally prepared to handle the rise and fall of stock prices in the market. If you find yourself unable to sleep well after a short-term drop in stock prices, then those stocks are not worth the stress.

Knowing your risk appetite will enable you to create a portfolio that suits your financial goals, personality and stick with it for the long haul.

If you don't want to do it yourself, the Robo-advisors take up the risk tolerance on your behalf and manage your investment portfolio.

Alternatively, you can seek the services of financial advisors who will help you to come up with a comprehensive financial plan that suits your portfolio. For example, when you create actively managed index funds, you can easily manage your funds to provide you with better risk-adjusted returns compared to other funds in the market.

Step 3: Choose your investment account and investments

Choosing an investment account is very important when building your portfolio. There are different types of accounts you can open to trade your stocks. You can go for a retirement account like IRA that works towards achieving your retirement goals and offer a tax advantage on the money invested.

Alternatively, if you're investing for a non-retirement goal, you can open a regular taxable brokerage account. You should always invest the money you don't need for the next five years in the stocks, otherwise you should go for a high-yield savings account.

It is important to know what you're investing in before you choose your investment account. You can use an online broker to help open your brokerage account or an IRA account.

After you open your investment account, you have to choose the different assets you want to invest in. Some of the assets you can invest include;

Stocks: If you expect the stocks of a certain company to go up and increase in value over time, you can invest in a portion of those stocks. Since the stocks are volatile, you're at high risk of incurring losses if the stocks lose value.

To mitigate this risk, you can invest in funds such as index funds, exchange-traded funds (ETFs), and mutual funds. It is good to allocate about 5% to 10% of individual stocks to your portfolio.

Mutual funds: Mutual funds are a great way to diversify your portfolio. They involve different types of securities, stocks, and funds you can choose from. Compared to individual stocks, mutual funds are less risky.

Additionally, some of the actively managed mutual funds have higher transaction fees and may not give you better returns like index funds which are passively managed. The index funds and the ETFs have lower transaction fees, and they try to match the performance of some companies within the S&P 500 index.

Bonds: A bond is a loan given to a company or government, and they usually pay back with interest over time. Though bonds offer fewer returns on investment, they are much safer than stocks. They're also referred to as fixed-income investments because you already know the amount of interest you receive from your investment.

Some of the factors you have to consider when evaluating the bonds include the credit rating, interest rate, maturity, and type of bond.

Step 4: Determine appropriate asset allocation

Now that you know what type of assets you want to invest in, you may find it challenging to choose how much you need to invest for each asset class. The process of splitting your portfolio to have different types of assets is called *asset allocation.*

Factors such as your current financial situation, future capital needs, and your risk tolerance contribute greatly to how to allocate different asset classes to your investment portfolio.

If you're in your 20s or 30's, you don't depend on your investments for income. In such cases, you can take higher-risk investments with expectations of higher returns. On the other hand, if you're almost your retirement age, your focus is investing in assets with lower risks. Most investors at this age tend to draw income from their investment in a tax-efficient manner.

Therefore, the higher the risk you can take, you can make your portfolio more aggressive. In such cases, you devote a large portion of your portfolio to stocks since you have more time to compound your returns. Otherwise, if you prefer a lower risk tolerance, you can go for a conservative portfolio which is associated with a short amount of investment time. So it is important to pick the type of stocks that satisfy your level of risk appetite.

Most financial advisors recommend those aged 30 years and above to allocate 70% to 80% of the portfolio to stocks and the remaining 20% to 30% of the portfolio to bonds or mutual funds. If you're 60 years, your portfolio shifts to allocating 50% to 60% to stocks and allocating the remaining 40% to 50% to bonds.

Step 5: Reassessing and rebalancing your portfolio

After creating your portfolio, you have to periodically analyze and rebalance it to accommodate the current price changes. The rise and fall of prices can affect the asset allocation of your portfolio, so rebalancing your portfolio is very important.

You should rebalance your portfolio after every 6 to 12 months. You can also do so after one of the asset class shifts more than the estimated percentage. For example, if you had estimated your portfolio to have 60% of stocks and they increase up to 65%, you should consider selling some of the stocks or consider investing in a different asset class until your stocks get back to the allocated 60%.

Some factors like your current financial situation, risk tolerance, and your future money needs may force you to adjust your asset allocation. If your risk tolerance reduces, you may consider reducing the number of stocks you hold. If you want to take up a great risk, you can allocate more volatile stocks to your investment portfolio.

So to rebalance your portfolio, you have to determine the overweighted and underweighted assets in your portfolio and how much of these assets you need to reduce or how you're going to allocate other asset classes.

Factors to consider when buying stocks

Putting your hard-earned money into different investments is not a guarantee you will be successful. Experienced investors do a lot of research before making any investment decisions. Research on different stocks and monitoring the daily ratings can help reduce the risk of losing your investment.

If you decide to purchase the stocks, there are a number of key factors you have to keep track of;

1. Price

When making investment decisions, price is one of the important factors you have to consider. Whether buying stocks, mutual funds, bonds, commodities, and real estate, you have to consider the price you pay for the investment. How much you pay for the investment determines whether the stock is a winning or losing bet.

Buy the stocks at the right prices, but how can you determine the right price for stocks? Investors have different ways to determine the right price, and most agree that you should buy stocks at a price lower than their future price. It is difficult to determine the future prices since you can't 100% predict what happens in the future.

So no matter how great the company is, it isn't worth it if you're not buying the shares of stocks at a good price. Even buying the stocks at the wrong time can also result in losses to your investment. You should always take advantage of the stock value before buying the stocks.

2. Intrinsic value of the company

According to Warren Buffet, you have to analyze the intrinsic value of the asset before buying and selling your investment. You can get the true value of the company by subtracting company liabilities from its assets. Alternatively, you can multiply the company's earnings per share with the annual growth rate to get the net worth of the company.

3. Stability

Stability is another factor you have to consider when looking for a suitable company to buy your stocks. All companies experience various economic conditions that affect the performance of the company. So before choosing stocks to invest in, evaluate the overall stability of the company despite the economic conditions.

4. Dividends

If the company is not stable, it will be difficult to pay dividends to the shareholders. So if the company has high yields, it is a sign of instability. If the company pays investors a lot of dividends, it's not good for investing because it doesn't reinvest its earnings.

A good company should be able to pay moderate and timely dividends to the shareholders. So don't choose stocks to invest in blindly.

5. Earnings growth

Looking at the company's annual net gains in income for a period of time helps you determine its earnings growth. Do the earnings increase rapidly? Though the prices may not change dramatically, you might have consistent and steady earnings from the company. Such a company will have better future growth.

6. Debt-to-equity ratio

Almost all companies carry a debt no matter the net wealth of the company. Therefore, be careful with companies that record a higher debt. Review the total liabilities of the company in its balance sheet and compare the company's debt to the equity ratio.

Buy stocks from a company that has more assets and few liabilities. If you're looking forward to investing in a company with a lower risk, then choose a company that has a debt to equity ratio of below 0.30.

7. Price-to-earnings (P/E) ratio

You have to compare the performance of stock prices in the market and relate this with the company's earnings. P/E ratio is an important factor when looking at the value of your investment and the fundamental analysis of the company.

The P/E ratio requires you to compare the current stock prices with its per-share earnings. To get the right figure, take the share price and divide it by earnings per share. The higher the ratio, the higher the returns in the future.

Tips for building a successful portfolio

1. Set clear objectives

Before you buy any stocks, you have to know the reasons why you want to invest and what are your expectations. Your objectives and investment goals provide you with the direction of what you should be doing. Otherwise, without clear set objectives, you will not have direction and purpose of what next.

Investment objectives should include factors such as capital appreciation, income, speculations, and capital preservation. There are different strategies you can use to achieve your investment goals.

For example, an investment portfolio that aims at increasing your income is totally different from an investment portfolio that helps you achieve capital appreciation. The two portfolios will never work the same under any timeline.

If your goals aren't clear, even if you use the best strategies and follow them to the latter, you will not be able to achieve the desired results. If you choose the wrong objective, you will end up being disappointed.

2. Reduce your investment turnover

As a rule of thumb, buy businesses instead of renting stocks. If you don't intend to hold the stocks for at least five years (owning a business), don't buy the shares unless you understand how volatile and irrational the stock market is for a short period of time.

Holding into your stocks for long has tax benefits. Profits from a long-term investment are subject to a lower tax rate compared to short-term investments. In addition, dividends from the long-term investment are also taxed at a low rate as compared to short-term stock addition in your portfolio. This is because short-term stocks always capitalize on the volatility of the stock market and are associated with the trading process rather than investing.

3. Take benefit of tax-shelter accounts

Low and middle-class individuals in the US can open retirement accounts with IRA and 401 (K). These accounts offer tax benefits to the members, but you have to follow the strict rules and a minimum contribution limit. If you withdraw money before your retirement age of 60, you have to pay a penalty tax though there are some exceptions.

You can take advantage of these tax benefit accounts and choose one that fits your investment goals and style. For example, you can invest in a variety of mutual funds using the 401(K) account. Employers often match your monthly contribution to this account.

The amount deducted from your taxable income is paid directly to your 401(K) account. You will pay taxes on the investment money once you withdraw it during your retirement age. The tax paid is usually lower since your income during retirement is very low.

If you're using an IRA account, your money will be taxed immediately; you make a contribution to the account and then enjoy a tax-free withdrawal after retirement. You will also not pay taxes on dividends, capital gains, and interest received from the money saved in your IRA account.

4. Reduce costs

Every dollar that you spend paying brokerage fee, commission, and other fund expenses lowers your investment capital. Though the amount of expenses you pay may be little, it accumulates over time.

Therefore, look for ways on how to reduce the costs in your investment portfolio. By the time you retire, you could have saved a couple of thousands or even millions of dollars.

5. Don't overpay on the assets

The market price of stocks is proportional to the returns you earn in your investment portfolio. Stocks prices fluctuate within a very short period of time, and sometimes, a good investment may be overpriced. Therefore, you have to do fundamental analysis prior to purchasing any shares.

By carrying out research on the company's financial performance and price fluctuation in the past and ensure you pay fair prices for the shares. On the other hand, if the stock prices are low and the company has low earnings yields, then don't expect to get more returns on your investment unless you're sure the company will turn around and grow significantly.

6. Diversify

One of the classic sayings on "don't put all your eggs in one basket," offers great advice to investors. That is, you should not put all your money under a single investment. Therefore, you should look for several high-quality stocks from different companies that provide steady dividends to invest in.

By diversifying your investment will help spread your risks across different industries, geographical regions, or companies with different management styles and performance. If a natural calamity affects industries in a particular region, its effects will only affect a portion of your portfolio.

Though you may feel its impact, it's not intense compared to if you had invested all your money in that geographical region or company.

Chapter Summary

Creating your investment portfolio doesn't have to be a complicated affair. With the above simple steps, you can create a more competitive portfolio. The most important factor is understanding your investment goals and coming up with investment strategies that align with the set goals.

Throughout the construction process of your investment portfolio, you have to keep in mind how to diversify your investments and how to pick the right asset classes for your portfolio.

In the next chapter, you will learn common mistakes young investors make.

Chapter Eight

Common Mistakes Young Investors Make

There are many misconceptions about stock investing that make amateur investors very reluctant to take that first big step to get into the market. Those who are willing to take the first step can make several mistakes if they don't spend the time necessary to educate themselves on how to properly invest first.

When I started investing, I had no idea what I was doing. There was a specific industry I felt was hugely undervalued and was quickly going to boom back to all-time highs. So what did I do as a new investor? I purchased high-dollar out of the money call option contracts that could've easily expired as worthless if I was wrong. What happened? Well, I actually made over a 300% return in the matter of a week. I was ecstatic! But it was all luck. I didn't know what I was doing. So I immediately took those profits, re-invested them and lost all of it over the period of the next three weeks. Even young, inexperienced investors can get lucky but only well-educated ones make money in the long-run.

A lot of these mistakes are very common and entirely avoidable.

Some of these mistakes include;

1. Procrastinating

Procrastination is a major mistake that young investors commonly make. Some of them believe they're too young to start investing or they need a lot of money to buy stocks. As a result, they keep postponing opening their first account. Don't let this be you!

The stock market is very volatile but you don't have to wait to perfectly time the market before you take action. No one can time the market perfectly. The best way to start your investment journey is to create a routine around it. You can start by putting aside some money each month for investments even if it is as little as a few hundred dollars.

Do not time the market by waiting for the stock prices to rise or fall so that you can start investing. Start as early as possible. The earlier you put money aside to work for you, the more money you will be able to accumulate years down the road.

If you start investing a few hundred dollars a month in an S&P 500 index ETF such as SPY as early as 25 then by the time you're 60 years, you will be a millionaire.

2. Failing to understand the businesses you're investing in

Warren Buffet warns investors against investing in companies they don't understand. You can avoid this by building a diversified portfolio of businesses and sectors you understand that consists of mutual funds and exchange-traded funds (ETFs).

If you intend to invest in individual stocks, you must research the company you want to buy your stocks from. Have a clear understanding of its business model and its value before buying the stocks. Know the company's financials, management strategies, unique advantages and balance sheet.

3. Lack of patience

When it comes to stock investing, patience is the key to growing your portfolio. Always follow a gradual and steady approach to building your portfolio and maximizing your returns.

Be realistic when building your portfolio. Don't expect your stocks to give you better yields in a very short period of time.

4. Speculative investing

This is another mistake young investors make because they believe taking huge risks will result in higher returns. Remember my story at the beginning of this chapter? One's age determines the amount of risk one should be willing to take. At age 25, you can take big risks with the expectation of big returns. This is because if you lose your investment, you will have enough time to recover it.

So most of the young investors tend to gamble on big returns. Instead of gambling and getting involved in speculative trades, as a young investor, you should only invest in companies that have higher risk and a higher potential for better returns in the long-term.

A higher percentage of small-cap stocks are associated with higher risks but also have higher return potential. Though the companies may seem less established, in the long run, they can become a household name with increasing stock values.

5. *Relying on too much leverage*

Any investor can take advantage of using leverage through margin. Trading with leverage means you pay for only a small percentage of the total purchase value for a stock and borrow the rest on credit through your brokerage firm. Leverage allows you to make higher returns with less upfront capital, however, it almost always involves higher risks. Just like dealing with highly speculative trades, leverage can destroy even the best investment portfolio.

A portfolio drop of about 20% to 25% may not have much impact on a young investor, but it could lead to a drop of much more if leverage is used or you get a margin call. You not only incur losses but may also become discouraged and assume a risk-averse position going forward.

To avoid such a case, you should moderately use leverage. Only allocate a portion of funds in the portfolio to leverage.

6. *Not doing enough research*

Young investors and beginners make this mistake. They make investment decisions without doing thorough research about the stocks they want to buy. The kind of information you research about the stocks depends on your investment goals, however there are some basic financial metrics you must understand about a company before investing.

Always look at a company's quarterly financial statements. In these, you must pay attention to their revenue, net income, earnings, earnings per share, trailing P/E, forward P/E, and return on equity. Make sure you understand how the company makes money, what its competitive advantage or economic moat is, and what the management teams plan for the future is.

If you don't have enough time to research the stock market and learn how to invest, you can hire financial advisors to handle the investment on your behalf.

Some other investors who don't want to ask questions and do the research on stocks choose to invest in index funds. This is a viable alternative because you can still make decent returns.

7. Letting your emotions control you

Fear and greed rule the stock market. If you let fear or greed control your investment decisions, you have set yourself up for failure. You must think about every trade from an objective standpoint to avoid making decisions out of panic or fear. Only make decisions once they are well thought out.

Though the stock market returns may deviate for very short periods of time, always be optimistic. Over the long term, the historical average returns are 10% for large-cap stocks.

Chapter Summary

Take the time to understand the companies that you invest in. Knowing the most common mistakes investors make and coming up with ways to avoid them will help you succeed.

Avoid gambling and focus your investment on companies that have a long-term upside. You should also know the type of investor you want to be so that you can ask yourself the right questions and do research that gets you what you need to make the right investment decisions.

Do not procrastinate; start your investment journey as soon as possible to generate more money.

Final Words

Investing in the stock market is one of the greatest ways to build your wealth in the long haul. Though the stock market is very volatile, proper research and following an appropriate investment strategy can help you reap huge benefits.

Stocks involve a lot of risks, and the higher the risks, the higher the returns. When you buy a company's stocks from the stock exchange, you have the right to receive the residual claims of that company in the form of capital gains and losses.

If you're a common shareholder of the company, you have the right to receive dividends from the company's revenues. Preference shareholders have limited rights in the company.

Some investors prefer to buy the stocks at a lower price, hold them for a while and sell when the prices increase, making a profit for their investment. Those who have experience in how the stock market works know how to take advantage of bull and bear markets.

If you're a beginner investor, you should start by setting up your investment goals. These will serve as a benchmark to compare your actual performance and your expectations.

Once you determine your investment goals, you need to analyze what type of investor you are. This requires you to evaluate your personality and come up with ways on how you will invest in stocks. This information will act as the basis for how you invest (day trading, swing trading, long-term investing), what you invest in (stocks, bonds, ETFs, cryptocurrency), and what your investment goals are.

Decide on the amount of money you want to put aside for buying stocks. Come up with a budget for how much money you will initially put into the stock market then set aside a small amount of funds to invest every single month. Over time this will allow your portfolio to grow into a nice nest egg.

Build your portfolio with individual stocks or decide to diversify your portfolio by including exchange-traded funds (ETFs). ETFs can be traded throughout the trading day and in the form of bonds, mutual funds, foreign current, commodities, and real estate.

You can decide to do it yourself or be passively involved. ETFs that track different indexes such as the S&P 500, Dow Jones, Nasdaq 100, and Russell 200 provide investment strategies that target specific industries. This helps you choose the best companies to invest your stocks in. Take advantage of the different types of ETFs to make the right investment decision.

Companies that are well established and have less long-term growth potential often pay higher dividends to the shareholders. Therefore, when building your portfolio, choose high-paying dividend stocks to grow your portfolio.

Dividends help you generate passive income, and diversifying your dividend portfolio will help you increase your income stream. Some of the strategies you can use include the use of Dividend Aristocrats and dividend kings, among others.

Value and growth investing strategies are great tools for building your portfolio. Experienced investors purchase stocks are able to identify companies that are undervalued with high overall growth potential. These strategies are widely recognized, and modern investors follow them to amass huge wealth from their investment.

Billionaire Warren Buffet, one of the most well-known value investors, uses this strategy to choose the best-undervalued stocks and hold them for the long term. Value investing focuses on buying a business rather than trading stocks.

Growth investing requires you to evaluate a company's potential for future growth and compare it with its intrinsic value. There are various strategies you can use to fully utilize the growth strategy and choose the best company to invest in. you can choose among different types of growth stocks in the market.

Your portfolio should have different types of asset classes so as to minimize the risks associated with the rise and fall of prices in the market. So how can you build a well-balanced portfolio? Our guide has different steps you can follow to set up your portfolio and determine an appropriate asset allocation.

Analyze your portfolio, and depending on your performance, you can decide what type of asset classes to increase and which to reduce from your portfolio.

Lastly, you have to learn some of the mistakes investors make and avoid them to have a successful investment.

References

What Drives the Stock Market? (n.d.).*Investopedia.* https://www.investopedia.com/articles/basics/04/100804.asp

What Determines a Company's Share Price? (n.d.). *Investopedia.* https://www.investopedia.com/ask/answers/061615/how-companys-share-price-determined.asp

The Wall-street. (2018). Trading Basics-Factors that Influence Share Prices. https://wall-street.com/trading-basics-factors-influence-share-prices/

Corporate Finance Institute (2020). Market Capitalization. https://corporatefinanceinstitute.com/resources/knowledge/finance/what-is-market-capitalization/

NerdWallet. (n.d.).Whoops, wrong turn! https://www.nerdwallet.com/article/investing/average-stock-market-return

Jason Hall, J.H. (2021) Average Stock Market Return. *The Motley Fool.* https://www.fool.com/investing/how-to-invest/stocks/average-stock-market-return/

What Is the Buy and Hold Strategy? (n.d.). *The Balance.* https://www.thebalance.com/what-is-buy-and-hold-2466543

Long Position Definition. (n.d.). *Investopedia.* https://www.investopedia.com/terms/l/long.asp

Short (Short Position) Definition. (n.d.). *Investopedia.* https://www.investopedia.com/terms/s/short.asp

An Overview of Bull and Bear Markets. (n.d.). *Investopedia.* https://www.investopedia.com/insights/digging-deeper-bull-and-bear-markets/

Frankel, MC. (2021). How to Invest in Stocks: A Beginners Guide for Getting Started. *The Motley Fool.* https://www.fool.com/investing/how-to-invest/stocks/

O'Shea, A. (2021). How to Invest in Stocks. *NerdWallet.* https://www.nerdwallet.com/article/investing/how-to-invest-in-stocks

Reinkensmeyer, B. (2021). Best Trading Platforms 2021. *StockBrokers.com.* https://www.stockbrokers.com/guides/online-stock-brokers

Edge, M. (n.d.). Getting to know exchange-traded funds. *Merrill Edge.* https://www.merrilledge.com/article/getting-to-know-exchange-traded-funds

7 Best ETF Trading Strategies for Beginners. (n.d.). *Investopedia.* https://www.investopedia.com/articles/investing/090115/7-best-etf-trading-strategies-beginners.asp

How To Pick The Best ETF. (n.d.). *Investopedia.* https://www.investopedia.com/articles/exchangetradedfunds/08/etf-choose-best.asp

Make the right ETF selection: tips and tricks. (n.d.). *JustETFAcademy.* https://www.justetf.com/uk/academy/make-the-right-etf-selection.html

O'Shea, A. (2021). What is a Dividend and How Do They Work? *NerdWallet.* https://www.nerdwallet.com/article/investing/what-are-dividends

Blake, B. (2018). Investing for Passive Income: 5Steps for Living Off Dividends Forever. *Medium.* https://medium.com/@info_78241/investing-for-passive-income-5-steps-for-living-off-dividends-forever-b24768053e03

Reynolds, B. (2020). The Snowball Effect: How To Compound Your Wealth Like Warren Buffet. *Sure Dividend.* https://www.suredividend.com/snowball-effect/

Warren Buffett: How He Does It. (n.d.). *Investopedia.* https://www.investopedia.com/articles/01/071801.asp

Investment Strategies To Learn Before Trading. (n.d.). *Investopedia.* https://www.investopedia.com/investing/investing-strategies/

Kalogeropoulos, D. (2021). Growth Investing: A Step-by-Step Guide for Getting Started. *The Motley Fool.*

https://www.fool.com/investing/stock-market/types-of-stocks/growth-stocks/how-to-invest/

A Beginner's Guide to Growth Investing. (n.d.). *Investopedia.* https://www.investopedia.com/articles/basics/13/introduction-to-growth-investing.asp

6 Secrets to Building a Successful Investment Portfolio. (n.d.). *The Balance* https://www.thebalance.com/six-secrets-to-building-a-successful-investment-portfolio-357834

Benson, A. (2021). Investment Portfolio: What It Is and How to Build a Good One. *NerdWallet.* https://www.nerdwallet.com/article/investing/investment-portfolio

Learn 4 Steps to Building a profitable Portfolio. (n.d.). *Investopedia.* https://www.investopedia.com/financial-advisor/steps-building-profitable-portfolio/

Factors to Consider When Buying stocks. (n.d.). *The Balance.* https://www.thebalance.com/factors-to-consider-when-analyzing-stocks-3140762

5 Common Mistakes Young Investors Make. (n.d.). *Investopedia.* https://www.investopedia.com/articles/younginvestors/09/common-mistakes-young-investors.asp

Printed in Great Britain
by Amazon